THE TOP FIVE THINGS TO CONSIDER BEFORE FILING AN EMPLOYEE RELATIONS COMPLAINT

And How to File An Effective Complaint

PATRICE MILLER

Copyright © 2018 Patrice Miller
All rights reserved
First Edition

PAGE PUBLISHING, INC.
New York, NY

First originally published by Page Publishing, Inc. 2018

ISBN 978-1-64298-480-4 (Paperback)
ISBN 978-1-64298-481-1 (Digital)

Printed in the United States of America

Preface

THIS BOOK WILL discuss many of the ins and outs of filing employee relations (ER) and equal employment opportunity (EEO) complaints in the workplace. Many complaints that are filed are often triggered by unresolved conflicts between employees and their coworkers or leaders; they generally do not meet the litmus test to rise to a company policy violation or illegal activity. According to the 2017 Ethics and Compliance Hotline and Incident Management Benchmark Report, the median rate of substantiated cases was 38 percent in 2016. In my experience, even some of those substantiated cases do not rise to the level of a company policy violation or illegal activity; some are unprofessional conduct or employee conflicts. This disappoints many employees that are filing ER and/or EEO complaints (i.e., harassment, discrimination, and retaliation complaints) because many are not substantiated and the employees end up believing that the system is flawed or the company is not genuinely sincere about a workplace free of harassment and discrimination. Knowing the difference can help you determine more likely than not whether your claim will be substantiated or not, which may save you from further frustration, or look at other avenues to resolve your issue.

Contents

Introduction 7

Chapter 1: Top Five Things to Consider before Filing
Your Complaint 9
Chapter 2: Chronic Complainers and Venting 15
Chapter 3: Workplace Bullying and Incivilities 20
Chapter 4: What Is Illegal Activity and Company Policy
Violations in the Workplace? 24
Chapter 5: Is It Illegal Activity, Policy Violation, or
Employee Conflict? 28
Chapter 6: Filing Effective and Ineffective Complaints 32
Chapter 7: Tips on Resolving Conflict 39

Summary 47
Appendix A 49
Notes 51

Introduction

BASED ON MY approximately twenty-plus years of experience in employee relations (ER) and equal employment opportunity (EEO), I have interacted with and investigated thousands of complaints. I'll start by defining employee relations (ER), and then EEO. According to an article titled "What Are Employee Relations?" from the HRZone website, *employee relations*, which was formerly known as industrial relations, "is concerned with the contractual, emotional, physical and practical relationship between employer and employee." With that, employee relations are always into play in the workplace, whether good or bad; with the bad typically resulting from unresolved conflicts. Scott (2009) puts this into perspective in saying that with two or more people in a workplace, there will very likely be conflict. The conflicts can range from minor quarrels about who drank the last cup of coffee and did not make a new pot to major disputes involving discrimination or sexual harassment. Anytime people interface, disagreements and disputes can result. This reminds me of when I first started doing employee relations and the person training me said if there are even only two people in a company, there will always be a need for employee relations. I learned he was right about that based on my subsequent years of experience! According to Muller (2014), human resources (HR) spends at least 24 percent of their time resolving employee relations problems.

Equal employment opportunity (EEO), according to the Equal Employment Opportunity Commission, refers to "laws that make it illegal to discriminate against a job applicant or an employee because of the person's race, color, religion, sex (including pregnancy, gender identity, and sexual orientation), national origin, age (forty or older), disability or genetic information. It is also illegal to discriminate against a person because the person complained about discrimination, filed a charge of discrimination, or participated in an employment discrimination investigation or lawsuit," or otherwise known as retaliation. This will be discussed in more detail in chapter 4.

While most large companies have ER and EEO departments and do genuinely want engaged employees to work in a workplace free of harassment and discrimination, much of their concern is wanting to mitigate risk and preserve their reputation.

I recall some employees asking me during our initial meeting to discuss their complaint, also referred to as an intake, "Are you here for me or the company?" I responded very politely, "While I am a neutral fact finder, at the end of the day, the company signs my paycheck." With that, even though company investigators are mostly described as neutral fact finders, companies, and understandably so, want to know where they stand from a risk-liability standpoint (i.e., how much money or reputation they stand to lose).

Thus, the law or illegal activity and company policy violations are of the company's utmost concern. Oftentimes, employee complaints do not rise to those levels, and many employees are disappointed when their case is not substantiated because it did not rise to illegal activity or policy violations. For the most part, many cases turn out to be about conflict resolution, which Muller (2014) states that HR managers spend anywhere from 24 percent to 60 percent trying to resolve workplace conflicts and that 22 percent of employees are disengaged because of those workplace conflicts. Many of the workplace conflicts turn out to be workplace incivilities and/or workplace bullying or simply an unskilled or poor manager. To minimize some of the disappointments and frustration of filing complaints that turn out not to be substantiated, this book gives five things to consider before filing a complaint and how to file an effective complaint.

CHAPTER 1

Top Five Things to Consider before Filing Your Complaint

1. What's really going on in my situation?
2. Does this rise to a policy violation or illegal activity?
3. How will filing my complaint affect me and my future career?
4. What's in it for me?
5. Is this something I can resolve before making this a formal complaint?

Number 1

WHAT'S REALLY GOING on in my situation (i.e., long-term conflict with someone, past anger and/or bitterness, etc., *or* illegal activity or company policy violation)?

In many cases, people file complaints when they are emotionally charged and have had it with their situation. They are no longer in the "take a step back and look at the situation in its entirety" mode.

They are often surprised when the investigator doesn't look quite as shocked as them when they are explaining their issue. For example, some have looked at me almost as if I could not have possibly heard what they said when I remain calm; the look on their face was as though they were thinking, *Didn't you just hear what I said they did to me?*

This calmness is primarily because the investigator has heard very many complaints and not a lot of things shock them *or* the complainant's issue has escalated so deeply within them and it feels worse to them than it really is. In general, the longer we focus on something, the larger it grows; hence, the old saying "Making a mountain out of a molehill" sometimes comes in to play. *Please keep in mind, I'm not saying this is everyone's issue, but I'm just saying—take a step back and look at it in its entirety,* even if you must write it down and be honest with yourself.

It is not uncommon that once a person is emotionally charged about something or someone—anything that anyone says about it or the person, whether positive or negative, comes across as negative—they sometimes lose sight of the big picture in the moment. In some cases, some will report that their suspect said hello to them and their perception was that there must be some ulterior motive by the suspect leading to something negative against the complainant. Because after all, as far as the complainant is concerned, there is no way the suspect was trying to make amends by saying hello. Surely, they must be up to something.

Finally, ask yourself how you are contributing to this issue and/or if you are the one that is actually behaving as a bully or a chronic complainer. I've seen that before too, where the complainant is really the bully and filing a complaint trying to distract from their own behavior, or are displaying behaviors of a chronic complainer. See characteristics of a chronic complainer in chapter 2 and the bullying checklist assessment in chapter 3.

Number 2

Does this rise to a policy violation or illegal activity based on the definitions given earlier?

Again, as mentioned in number 1, take a step back. Does it meet illegal activity or a company policy violation? For example, if

THE TOP FIVE THINGS TO CONSIDER BEFORE FILING AN EMPLOYEE RELATIONS COMPLAINT

the issue is between you and your coworker disagreeing or clashing on some specific issues, at work or personal, especially if it is personal, is this an issue that needs conflict-resolution support (see chapter 5 for tips on handling conflict resolution) or possibly some mediation by your leader or, in some cases, human resources (HR)? Again, many employees end up very disappointed and sometimes very upset because their complaint is not substantiated because it does not rise to a policy violation or illegal activity and feel that they have no options for resolutions. Typically, conflict resolution or employee disputes do not rise to illegal activity or policy violations around harassment or discrimination. It is also important to understand that unequal treatment in the workplace does not always mean unlawful treatment. Recognize that the employer's actions may be, or at least feel, totally unfair, but it is not necessarily unlawful. A summary of EEO laws is in chapter 4.

Keep in mind that, if it is a conflict or clash, it will take both parties to resolve the dispute, and most importantly, be mindful that one's unwillingness to participate in resolving the issues versus having someone else resolve it for them can actually begin to move them toward formal coaching plans, performance improvement plans, and ultimately, a disciplinary situation leading to termination because they have now refused to cooperate or have become insubordinate to work direction. Try not to let your pride get the best of you.

Number 3

How will filing your complaint affect you and your future career?

This is an important question. As you know, retaliation for filing complaints is prohibited by law (federal, state, and local) and company policies (see chapter 4). However, many consider the rudimentary definition of *retaliation* like an eye for an eye versus how the law and policies define *retaliation* as an adverse term or condition of employment based on nonbusiness reasons occurring subsequent to them filing their complaint.

For example, an employee filed a complaint of harassment against their leader, and subsequently, their performance rating was lowered even though this employee had always received good ratings. This would be investigated as a retaliation complaint. However, if this employee got the same rating before and after filing a complaint, there is no obvious adverse action that occurred, because nothing changed.

Additionally, keep in mind, before filing your complaint, leaders above your leader are notified of the complaint, which, in most cases, is a positive. However, if you are constantly filing multiple complaints that are not merited, remember, you're dealing with human beings, and it is human nature to become defensive when constantly having to respond to complaints against them. Additionally, I have yet to see in my many years of experience anyone's career moves in an upward direction after filing numerous complaints that are not substantiated and are mostly around unresolved conflicts. Also, I'll tell you a little secret: this person is likely very well-known by their peers, HR, the law department, and higher-level leaders in your area and, possibly, enterprise-wide.

Finally, being one who has responded to numerous complaints and having raised complaints on behalf of myself and others, it can be *very emotionally draining* with the interviews, questioning, and responding to others' allegations of your conduct. Because believe me, whatever you have done even close to inappropriate, the suspect or a witness will be bringing it up, whether accurate or twisted. So be warned: if you do have any skeletons in the closet, are you okay with having them come out of the closet? I'm just saying; just know it is likely coming. Of course, this is not to stop people from filing a complaint in and of itself—it is simply a warning.

Number 4

What's in it for me?

What is the true motive for filing this complaint? Do they truly, or in good faith, believe they have been treated inappropriately, or are they out to get someone they have a conflict with in trouble? I have seen many of the latter of these, and many of them come in the form of anonymous complaints and are generally vague and verbally attacking someone. If this is the case, they won't be satisfied with the outcome. Most often than not, those are not substantiated, and now you have started to put fuel on a long-standing conflict with the individual, which often negatively affects you and your coworkers and the morale of the entire team.

Also, remember, if you are out to get them terminated, even if the complaint is substantiated, as long as it is not egregious, they will likely not be terminated; if the inappropriate behavior stops, that is usually considered as it being addressed. So if that is your motive, don't get too bent out of shape when you're told the issue has been addressed and you go back to work and they are still sitting there. However, if the motive is in good faith, and to have some inappropriate behavior addressed, that's a good reason to move forward.

Number 5

Is this something I can resolve before making this a formal complaint?

It is always best to be able to solve an issue before it becomes formal. It adds so much to the employee's competencies in communication and conflict resolution, and the employee can be viewed as a high performer around resolving conflicts and viewed as an informal or formal leader on the team. This can be very empowering and a boost to one's confidence and skill set. In addition, it can help keep the morale up on the team instead of dragging the whole team into the issue.

Finally, while it is important to speak up, Lucas (2016) offers the following things to think through before filing your complaint or going to HR.

You've done nothing to solve the problem yourself. While HR works to keep an engaged workforce and minimize workplace distraction, they are not there to handle every conflict that comes up between coworkers. For example, if your coworker chomps on gum all day, driving you to distraction, you'll likely be more successful if you mentioned it to them first.

When you're actually the problem. If your complaint is that your boss is mean, before you show up in the HR department, ask yourself what the real problem is. It's not mean if your boss tells you that you must be on time to work, take only thirty minutes or one hour for lunch, and get your work done. Likewise, if you're upset that your coworker got the promotion and you didn't yet he/she does twice the work you do, going to HR won't help your case.

When you haven't done your homework. If you think your salary is too low, you should have some pretty good evidence before you come in. For example, if your official job description is not reflective of what you actually do, do you have information that shows that people in similar jobs do the same work and make more money than you do?

You want other people to change. We all want other people to change instead of changing ourselves, but if the problem isn't actually a legal one, you're going to have far better luck if you come to HR with the question of "What can I do differently?" rather than "Can you make someone else behave differently?"

In sum, it is always best if you can address the issue early on before it grows out of control. It reduces the stress that mounts on you and the cost and time for those involved, including HR, witnesses that are interviewed, leaders having to spend time intervening, etc., which can sometimes stir the pot even more than the original issues for all involved and make matters worse. Most importantly, make sure you check yourself to ensure you are part of the solution, not the problem. In other words, be sure you are trying to resolve the issues and not becoming what can be perceived as a chronic complainer or a workplace bully.

CHAPTER 2

Chronic Complainers and Venting

Chronic Complainers

As mentioned earlier in chapter 1, when someone files numerous complaints, they are well-known by their peers, HR, the law department, and leaders of their department.

With that, this is by no means to discourage you from filing complaints when warranted.

This section is to help support people's self-awareness of their own behavior, which can help them file an effective complaint versus being perceived as a chronic complainer.

According to an article in *Psychology Today* (August 2015) titled "No One Likes a Complainer," *some complaints are totally justified. Others just lead to self-sabotage.* The title itself is pretty accurate, based on my years of experience. The article states the following characteristics that make up a complainer:

- *Nothing seems good enough.*
- *You always must be right and no one can challenge you—it is harassment if they do.*
- *You're a little perplexed by those who seem cheery most of the time.*

For chronic complainers, each situation becomes an opportunity to find fault. Eventually, this drains life of pleasure. Chronic complaining can also affect one's mood by producing a negative mood state or, sometimes, depression. Thus, the chronic complainer falls into a perpetual cycle of finding fault, feeling negative, and then being unable to face the next situation with an open mind. The following illustrations show what can happen to the chronic complainer:

What Can We Do about Chronic Complaining?

Here are three questions to ask yourself:

1. Is my complaint specific and limited or general and unclear? Unclear and general complaints usually refer to problems that have no solution, like the weather.
2. Are your complaints the same ones over and over? It may be that your complaints are a way of getting attention or an indirect way of asking for help.
3. Are you afraid that if you don't focus on the negative in a situation, you will be unprepared for a major disappoint-

THE TOP FIVE THINGS TO CONSIDER BEFORE FILING AN EMPLOYEE RELATIONS COMPLAINT

ment? This strategy prevents a person from fully experiencing the positive aspects a situation may offer (*Psychology Today*, August 2015).

If you find you may have some characteristics of a chronic complainer, perhaps you may want to rethink the issues and review the top five things to consider before filing your complaint in chapter 1.

In some cases, people are not chronic complainers; sometimes they need to simply vent and really don't want any action taken. This is fine if, again, it is not dealing with law or policy violations. Let's talk about venting next.

Venting

According to the Free Dictionary by Farlex, *venting* is a "forceful expression or release of pent-up thoughts or feelings." Additionally, Dubois (2011) states in her article, "We think of venting as a transfer of heat; as 'blowing off steam,' meaning anger, which would otherwise stay inside, creating pressure which could cause us to explode at an inopportune moment. Venting is different than complaining, which means voicing a concern with the goal of changing something or addressing the cause of the problem."

It has both positive and negative aspects. Generally, it's better to let things out than hold them in, and doing so can feel almost like problem-solving—at least in the moment. Venting your frustrations alleviates tension and stress. You almost always feel better—as if you had a weight lifted off your shoulders—after sharing some perceived threat, misfortune, or injustice. However, constant venting with no action taken can turn into whining, which rarely resolves anything. It can also lead to self-limiting and self-defeating behaviors, like a victim. Oftentimes, it can become an excuse for *not* acting to resolve a problem or confront an issue that requires confrontation.

For example, if the company investigator must continually interrupt you to get back on focus, this may be more venting than lodging a specific complaint, which is okay as long as it is not constant and you are doing something to try resolving the issue. Finally, remember the following quote (author unknown):

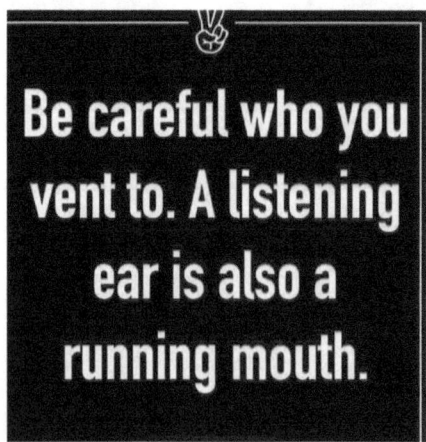

**THE TOP FIVE THINGS TO CONSIDER BEFORE
FILING AN EMPLOYEE RELATIONS COMPLAINT**

Be sure to manage how and how often you may be venting and whom you are venting to. While everyone we vent to does not necessarily have a running mouth, this can be possible, depending on who it is, so just be careful!

CHAPTER 3

Workplace Bullying and Incivilities

Workplace Bullying

ANOTHER HOT TOPIC that triggers complaints is the infamous workplace bully. This is also a complaint that often comes up not substantiated primarily because the behavior is subtle and often the suspect is an equal opportunity bully. So to show that you are being singled out from others is always difficult because they treat others the same way too, and to show that the behavior is clearly an illegal activity or a policy violation can be a challenge, even though the work environment may feel very uncomfortable.

Nonetheless, the issue should still be raised because if there is any inappropriate or unprofessional behavior occurring, it must be put to a stop since it can be costing the company low employee morale and thus low productivity and thus the bottom line, money—which, according to Parris (2014), can cost businesses up to $180 million annually. Always keep in mind that companies hire us to help provide a high-quality product and service for the company, to bring in profits and be paid for that service, not spend lots of money and time dealing with workplace bullies.

Before filing the complaint, you may want to do a self-check on whether you are displaying bullying behaviors. Make sure you are not conducting bullying behavior and are part of the problem,

THE TOP FIVE THINGS TO CONSIDER BEFORE FILING AN EMPLOYEE RELATIONS COMPLAINT

not the solution. Following is a quiz, developed by Hilary Holladay (2013), with minor changes, to help you determine whether you are contributing to the issue.

Award yourself one bully blast 💣 for each *yes* answer to the following questions:

- Have you ever snubbed a colleague or ignored his/her request for a meeting?
- Have you yelled at someone in your office or sent them an angry email?
- Have you ever gotten so close to a coworker during a dispute that he/she couldn't get past you?
- Have you followed a colleague down the hall while speaking angrily at him?
- Have you worked behind the scenes to prevent someone from getting a promotion or a raise in pay?
- Have you tried to exclude a qualified colleague from an important committee or project?
- Have you ambushed someone in a meeting with a question or remark designed to embarrass him/her in front of others?
- Have you twisted a colleague's words to make him/her look bad or made a fuss over a minor infraction just to get him/her in trouble?
- Have you denied a coworker credit for a job well done?
- Have you ever tried to turn other staff members against a colleague you dislike?

If you're holding even one bully blast 💣—that is, if you answered *yes* to even one of these questions—you may be a bully, no matter what your title.

If you do conduct yourself in this manner, aim to stop immediately. Get rid of the plotting, scheming, being rude, and criticizing others. And remember that you don't have to fight every battle or try to hold someone else back so you can get ahead. Understand that another person's success doesn't mean you're a failure. Acknowledge that bullying is a sign you're unhappy with yourself. Maybe it's time to do something about that. If you find that you are not likely a bully, there is one more area for you to examine yourself to be sure you are not part of the problem, which is *workplace incivilities*.

Workplace Incivilities

Workplace incivility according to Wikipedia, the free dictionary, is "low-intensity peculiar behavior with ambiguous intent to harm the target. Uncivil behaviors are regarded as characteristically rude and discourteous, showing a lack of concern for others." Incivility is less intense than workplace bullying, but it is more prevalent in companies. The most common uncivil behaviors include indifference to a worker's opinion, ignoring a coworker, and intimidating others. Although incivility is at the low end of the workplace-mistreatment continuum, it may not be ignored or overlooked because of the adverse impacts it can ultimately have on the company (Bibi, Zainab, Karim, Jahanvash, and Siraj up Din, *Pakistan Journal of Psychological Research* [Winter 2013], 317–334).

Below is a scale based on the articles by the authors above and my own experience. The scale describes typical uncivil behaviors, one or two of which, embarrassingly, I must say I have done something similar to before learning about incivilities. This is an appropriate time to check yourself, to see whether you have conducted uncivil behaviors. So like the workplace bully assessment, give yourself an incivility blast 💣 for each *yes* answer.

1. Avoided consulting someone when you would have normally been expected to do so.
2. Talked about someone or gossiped behind their back.
3. Was excessively slow in returning phone messages or emails without good reason for the delay.
4. Used an inappropriate tone when speaking to someone.

THE TOP FIVE THINGS TO CONSIDER BEFORE FILING AN EMPLOYEE RELATIONS COMPLAINT

5. Was unreasonably slow in dealing with matters that were important to someone's work.
6. Opened someone's desk drawers and/or took items without prior permission.
7. Publicly discussed someone's confidential personal information.
8. Spoke to someone in an aggressive tone of voice.
9. Intentionally failed to pass on information that someone should have been made aware of.
10. Made snide remarks about someone.
11. Took something from someone's desk without later returning it.
12. Read communications addressed to someone else, such as emails and faxes.
13. Raised your voice while speaking to someone.
14. Did not consult someone about a decision they should have been involved in.
15. Rolled your eyes at someone.

Basically, in my opinion, if you answered *no* to all these, you are good. However, if you had one or two incivility blasts, you may want to do a self-check in those areas. If you had three-plus incivility blasts, you should do some deeper digging on yourself; you may very well be a part of the problem and need to make some modification in your behavior.

CHAPTER 4

What Is Illegal Activity and Company Policy Violations in the Workplace?

WHILE THERE ARE many laws that can come into play in a workplace, the focus here is on laws and company policies related to EEO and employee relations investigations.

Illegal Activity

Following are EEO-related laws according to the Equal Employment Opportunity Commission US website. (Subject to Change)

Title VII of the Civil Rights Act of 1964 (Title VII)

This law makes it illegal to discriminate against someone on the basis of race, color, religion, national origin, or sex. (This includes sexual harassment.) The law also makes it illegal to retaliate against a person because the person complained about discrimination, filed a charge of discrimination, or participated in an employment discrimination investigation or lawsuit. The law also requires that employers reasonably accommodate applicants' and employees' sincerely held religious practices, unless doing so will impose an undue hardship on the operation of the employer's business.

THE TOP FIVE THINGS TO CONSIDER BEFORE FILING AN EMPLOYEE RELATIONS COMPLAINT

The Pregnancy Discrimination Act

This law amended Title VII to make it illegal to discriminate against a woman because of pregnancy, childbirth, or a medical condition related to pregnancy or childbirth. The law also makes it illegal to retaliate against a person because the person complained about discrimination, filed a charge of discrimination, or participated in an employment discrimination investigation or lawsuit.

The Equal Pay Act of 1963 (EPA)

This law makes it illegal to pay different wages to men and women if they perform equal work in the same workplace. The law also makes it illegal to retaliate against a person because the person complained about discrimination, filed a charge of discrimination, or participated in an employment discrimination investigation or lawsuit.

The Age Discrimination in Employment Act of 1967 (ADEA)

This law protects people who are forty or older from discrimination because of age. The law also makes it illegal to retaliate against a person because the person complained about discrimination, filed a charge of discrimination, or participated in an employment discrimination investigation or lawsuit.

Title I of the Americans with Disabilities Act of 1990 (ADA)

This law makes it illegal to discriminate against a qualified person with a disability in the private sector and in state and local governments. The law also makes it illegal to retaliate against a person because the person complained about discrimination, filed a charge of discrimination, or participated in an employment discrimination investigation or lawsuit. The law also requires that employers reasonably accommodate the known physical or mental limitations of an otherwise qualified individual with a disability who is an applicant or employee, unless doing so will impose an undue hardship on the operation of the employer's business.

Sections 102 and 103 of the Civil Rights Act of 1991

Among other things, this law amends Title VII and the ADA to permit jury trials and compensatory and punitive damage awards in intentional discrimination cases.

Sections 501 and 505 of the Rehabilitation Act of 1973

This law makes it illegal to discriminate against a qualified person with a disability in the federal government. The law also makes it illegal to retaliate against a person because the person complained about discrimination, filed a charge of discrimination, or participated in an employment discrimination investigation or lawsuit. The law also requires that employers reasonably accommodate the known physical or mental limitations of an otherwise qualified individual with a disability who is an applicant or employee, unless doing so will impose an undue hardship on the operation of the employer's business.

The Genetic Information Nondiscrimination Act of 2008 (GINA) Effective November 21, 2009

This law makes it illegal to discriminate against employees or applicants because of genetic information. Genetic information includes information about an individual's genetic tests and the genetic tests of an individual's family members, as well as information about any disease, disorder, or condition of an individual's family members (i.e., an individual's family medical history). The law also makes it illegal to retaliate against a person because the person complained about discrimination, filed a charge of discrimination, or participated in an employment discrimination investigation or lawsuit.

THE TOP FIVE THINGS TO CONSIDER BEFORE FILING AN EMPLOYEE RELATIONS COMPLAINT

State and Local Laws

State laws are stricter than federal laws; for example, the federal law in Title VII does not include sexual orientation, where most state or local laws do include sexual orientation.

California is probably one of the most, in my opinion, employee-friendly states and has more stringent laws than other states. The HR Certification Institute (HRCI) even has a separate professional certification for California (CA) from other states in the United States; the designation is PHR-CA instead of the PHR that is used for all other states. To find your state/local laws, the following link may be helpful: http://statelaws.findlaw.com/civil-rights-laws.html.

Company Policy Violations

Many company policies are contained in the employee code of conduct handbook and include the federal, state, and local laws. Employers have code of conduct polices specific to their organization, however, many codes of conducts have common policies, such as conflict of interest, using company equipment/property for personal use, false time reporting, etc. Some include workplace bullying, hazing, and in some cases, workplace incivilities, which, again, can be tricky to prove. Additionally, some will reference the company's vision/mission statements to treat all with dignity and respect; however, the definition of *respect* is very subjective and often does not rise to a policy violation.

CHAPTER 5

Is It Illegal Activity, Policy Violation, or Employee Conflict?

WHICH OF THE following scenarios would likely be a policy violation, illegal activity, or employee conflict?

Scenario 1

My coworker is harassing me—she won't pick up all the mail when it comes in as she is responsible to do; she will only get hers and leave mine sitting in the mail bin. Also, we are both responsible for answering the phone; however, she will not answer the phone when I am present in the office—she waits for me to answer.

Which of the following would you consider for this scenario?

A. Illegal activity and/or company policy violation
B. Employee conflict, not an illegal activity or a company policy violation leader should address

Scenario 2

My leader retaliated against me because I called him out on a mistake he made in a meeting, and then in a subsequent meeting, he called me out on a bigger error, which was very embarrassing, in front of the team and guest participants of the meeting.

Is this retaliation?

    A. Yes
    B. No

Scenario 3

I am not being promoted based on my age. There have been several promotions in the past year, and I am over age forty and the only one not given the opportunity to move up. I've been told that the younger generations are the ones that are up on the latest technology, which I find puzzling because I love keeping up with modern technology.

    A. Illegal activity and/or company policy violation
    B. Employee conflict, not an illegal activity or a company policy violation leader should address

Scenario 4

Your coworker has pictures of scantily dressed women on his desk and refers to them frequently out loud and in a derogatory manner when talking with his male coworkers.

    A. Illegal activity and/or company policy violation
    B. Employee conflict, not an illegal activity or a company policy violation leader should address

Scenario 5

Your leader has a large tattoo of a racially derogatory symbol on his arm and refuses to cover it up.

A. Illegal activity and/or company policy violation
B. Employee conflict, not an illegal activity or a company policy violation their leader should address

Scenario 6

Some of your coworkers have large signage of their choice of political party on their T-shirts or vehicles in a manner that includes derogatory religious slurs and offensive to others.

A. Illegal activity and/or company policy violation
B. Employee conflict, not an illegal activity or a company policy violation leader should address

Scenario 7

A coworker, who seems like a bully, challenges your idea in a meeting, and the discussion becomes very heated and you were offended; however, there was no inappropriate language used or physical altercation.

A. Illegal activity and/or company policy violation
B. Employee conflict, not an illegal activity or a company policy violation leader should address

Scenario 8

Your leader has a habit of winking at you and touching you in a way (e.g., rubbing your shoulders) that makes you feel uncomfortable.

A. Illegal activity and/or company policy violation
B. Employee conflict, not an illegal activity or a company policy violation leader should address

Answers to the scenarios are in Appendix A.

THE TOP FIVE THINGS TO CONSIDER BEFORE FILING AN EMPLOYEE RELATIONS COMPLAINT

Check out how you scored. This exercise may also help you in ensuring you file an effective complaint.

* * * * *

In summary, whether employee conflict, illegal activity, or a company violation, bringing issues forth is not easy; however, the earlier it is addressed, the easier it is resolved, especially with employee conflicts. When it comes to a formal complaint, oftentimes, the individuals have been putting up with their situation for a while and have pent-up frustration and anger that can escalate into something that is sometimes irreparable. Bottom line: you should address your issues early on if you can, because when it becomes a formal complaint, you have now formally complained about and, in some cases, accused the suspect in front of HR, your leader and your suspect's leaders, and any other witnesses that are interviewed. Things can become more uncomfortable than one thinks and sometimes never go back to what one hoped it would after filing a complaint; it's human nature. So if you are going to go that route, remember to look at the bigger picture, examine yourself, and make sure you make it an effective complaint. The next chapter will describe effective and ineffective complaints.

CHAPTER 6

Filing Effective and Ineffective Complaints

Effective Complaint

ACCORDING TO SELIG (2012) and Juliano (2015), an *effective complaint* is directed at a specific event, situation, or service that does not meet the person's expectations. It is one that is heard by the person at whom it is aimed and has a result that satisfies the complainant. The person bringing this complaint forth typically knows how to effectively ask for and obtain what they want.

The following are a few ways to help make your complaint effective:

- Know what you want to achieve. The most effective complainants are those who have a clear idea of what they want to achieve from their complaint and who set it out clearly to the person to whom they are complaining.
- When possible, identify the person who has the power to make the changes you seek, then complain to that person directly before filing a formal complaint through the company's designated procedure.

THE TOP FIVE THINGS TO CONSIDER BEFORE FILING AN EMPLOYEE RELATIONS COMPLAINT

- If possible, for ER complaints, voice one issue at a time. Too many issues will overwhelm the listener. What's really important to you? Focus on that first. I have had complainants come in with thirty-plus pages of documentation with issues that have happened in the past five to ten years, which can sometimes be TMI (too much information), untimely[1], and not relevant to the actual complaint. Additionally, when you tell the same vague story repeatedly and the investigator tries to get you to focus on something factual and you go back around to the same story, that's too much—it is too overwhelming, and we're not getting anywhere, which is ineffective. Remember to be brief, specific, and to the point. Prepare precise documentation.
- Lay out clear impacts or consequences if the complaint is not resolved, both positive and negative.
- Go through your company's designated complaint procedure versus sending random emails to the entire chain of command of your business unit or company; you'll likely get a more reasonable result that way. Remember, while you may get a quicker response because you send it to the CEO, it still may not be the response you want—and oh, by the way, as mentioned earlier in the last chapter, if it is not an effective complaint and you are filing multiple complaints that are of the same or similar issue, you can now add them to the list of people who know you well in the complaint arena and not so much in the light of an exceptional performance accomplishment you achieved. Based on my experience, if your case involves illegal activity and/or a policy violation, HR will address it and in no uncertain terms ignore it until it goes to the CEO.

---

[1] For the EEOC, "in general, you need to file a charge within 180 calendar days from the day the discrimination took place. The 180 calendar day filing deadline is extended to 300 calendar days if a state or local agency enforces a law that prohibits employment discrimination on the same basis" (https://www.eeoc.gov/employees/timeliness.cfm). Companies tend to follow the same standard.

- Write it down beforehand to organize your thoughts. It will help keep you on track and minimize going off track and cause your complaint to become vague and convoluted.
- Keep in mind that if you think through the big picture and have succinct and concise documentation, the investigation will go much smoother. You'll notice there hasn't been discussion on succinct and concise notes, so I'll note it here. Please have clear documentation of the complaint focused specifically on the issue, the impact, and your desired outcome, which can likely be done in three pages or less, depending on the circumstances. When you start hitting several pages, unless it is actual evidence, it is an appropriate time to stop and make sure the focus is not getting lost and it is becoming an ineffective complaint. For example, if you find yourself including in the actual complaint things that happened ten-plus years ago, it may be untimely (over one year) and therefore not considered for an investigation. Focus on recent events. Otherwise, the focus for the investigator may not only be whether the complaint is timely but will also be "Have you brought this up before?" and "Why are you just now bringing this forward?" It is important to note that for some investigators, including me, it can be challenging trying to figure out what to investigate in a vague complaint and/or wading and weeding through a bunch of irrelevant documentation, particularly going back years ago, trying to find the complaint that actually needs to be investigated!.
- Remain as calm as you can. When you are angry, things sometimes get said that should not be said. The focus may go to your anger, and sometimes it may even appear as though you are the problem. Again, keep in mind the specific issue and the result you want to achieve.
- Admit your part of the problem if you do have some liability in the matter. Your honesty will reflect positively on

THE TOP FIVE THINGS TO CONSIDER BEFORE FILING AN EMPLOYEE RELATIONS COMPLAINT

you, make your claims more believable, and perhaps even inspire some resolution.
- Again, I can't say this too much, resist the temptation to become a chronic complainer—you may slide over the slippery slope of self-sabotage or victimhood. Choose your issues. Some complaints, if they are not potential law or policy violations or do not have an impact on the work group, are simply not worth your time and trouble. Let them go!

Finally, speaking up about a complaint effectively and attaining a resolution can be personally empowering, can boost your self-esteem, and can enhance your feelings of effectiveness, bringing a sense of satisfaction that you were heard. Ultimately, it will support an engaging and productive work environment, which can make going to work more comfortable and even desirable for the whole team. The following is an example of an effective complaint:

Effective Complaint

Issue/allegation(s)—what happened?
- My leader retaliated against me by demoting me after I filed an EEO harassment complaint against him that was substantiated.
- Any other specific details of the event.

Who was involved?
- My leader (name), his leader (name), and any other witnesses (names).

When did this occur?
- Approximately three weeks after I filed the EEO harassment complaint, which I filed about two months ago.

How and/or how often has this occurred?
- My leader and his leader called me in the office and said, "Due to your declining performance, you are being demoted." He gave no explanation or legitimate business reason for this action.
- This has only happened on this one occasion; however, I know of him conducting this same behavior with others who have filed complaints (be prepared to include the who, what, when, where, and how).

Why do you think this happened?
- I think my leader got in trouble because of the complaint I filed. Since I filed, he barely speaks to me anymore.

How would you like to see this resolved?
- I would like my position back with any back pay I may have missed.

THE TOP FIVE THINGS TO CONSIDER BEFORE FILING AN EMPLOYEE RELATIONS COMPLAINT

Ineffective Complaint

The ineffective complaint is different altogether. The topic of the complaint is generally one that the complainant has little control over. However, by complaining about it, the individual gets the sense of gaining some control and, erroneously, feels mastery over something that cannot be mastered. Ineffective complaints are usually lodged by those who often see the glass as half-empty to protect themselves from disappointment, and oftentimes, when the glass is viewed as half-empty, nothing seems to have a positive outlook. I have met many where no matter what suggestions are made to help resolve their issues, according to them, they won't work out, and in some cases, they are ultimately out for revenge against someone. In fact, for some, unless you are going to help them get revenge, you are of no real use to them.

In addition, the ineffective complaints are vague and oftentimes come in as anonymous with little information, giving the investigator no place to begin an investigation. For example, statements are given like "Everyone else comes in late, but I'm the only one the manager talks to about it" *or* "My coworkers are not meeting goals either, but the manager never talks to them and lets them take long lunches but wants me to come back earlier." Most of the time, when they are asked *how they know the manager hasn't said anything to anyone else*, they do not have any solid evidence or response.

The ineffective complainer, when asserting a specific complaint, often does so in a way that nearly guarantees they will not get their needs met. This person believes that they will be frustrated. So without realizing it, they use tactics that put people on the defensive. For example, they may behave childishly or like a bully when lodging a complaint and make unrealistic demands or may bring it up at the wrong time in front of others inappropriately. When they don't get what they want, the belief that they can never get satisfaction is reinforced. In the long run, they are likely attracting their own misery and unhappiness in the workplace.

Finally, it is important to always remember that most EEO/ER company investigators are *neutral fact finders*. They do not *represent the employee*. You may ask why this is here. Some employees believe when they file a complaint, they have just obtained a company attorney to represent them—they have not! They have simply initiated a complaint for a neutral fact finder that is paid by the company to investigate their complaint.

Also, seasoned investigators are very used to someone saying they have an attorney. This does not change anything from someone who has an attorney or doesn't. The investigation is still conducted in the same manner. If it reaches the company's legal department, an attorney can likely make a difference in how things are conducted at that point.

Summary

Once you look at the big picture by considering all the above (i.e., chronic complaining, workplace bullying, workplace incivilities, effective or ineffective complaints), then decide whether you should go ahead with filing a formal complaint or determine if your situation is an employee conflict. Chapter 7 will cover some tips on resolving conflict.

CHAPTER 7

Tips on Resolving Conflict

ACCORDING TO SCOTT (2009, p. 11), "Understand what's behind the conflict, get beyond the surface issues, and work to find satisfying resolutions for everyone involved."

Keep in mind the other person's point of view and consider outlying factors that may be creating or provoking problems, like group dynamics or workplace norms. Speculation based on limited or selective information causes miscommunication, misunderstanding, and ultimately, conflict.

Remember, people can look at the same picture and see something different; things are not always seen until they are pointed out (see picture below). Thus, start with an open mind, and you may find some common ground.

PATRICE MILLER

How many figures can you see in the image below?

Answer: If you look closely, you can see both a young and an elderly woman.
This picture, My Wife and My Mother-in-Law, is a good example of two images existing in one, and was published in 1915 by the cartoonist W.E. Hill.

Having good conflict-resolution skills is very important and can come in handy since most or any complaint is based on conflict or disagreement. Some things to keep in mind when trying to resolve conflict: First, remember to take a deep breath and count to ten—this always helps. I experienced this working while in the doctor's office. My blood pressure was very high. The nurse had left the room, and when the doctor came in, he said he wanted to take it again. He held my arm and said, "Take a deep breath," almost taking a deep breath with me at the same time. He took my blood pressure again, and it was 120/80! So taking a deep breath does help. Think about and examine exactly what the conflict is objectively. Additionally, try to pick an appropriate time and place to address it, especially if it happened in the heat of a moment. Give yourself time to calm down, pull yourself away, and then regroup.

Additionally, Maxwell (2007) says that in conflict management, confrontation is the way to resolution. While this is not always comfortable, he offers four steps to get to the objective: (1) be clear and direct, (2) don't draw attention to yourself, (3) lay out the issue and ask for a decision, and (4) trust God or your higher self to justify and reveal the truth. Following these steps may help in your approach to resolving the conflict.

With this, knowing how to confront conflict is also very important. The Thomas-Kilmann Conflict Mode Instrument (2007) describes ways people respond to conflict; being familiar with these responses and knowing how you might be responding may help with this. They note five different methods of responding to conflict:

1. Competing
2. Collaborating
3. Compromising
4. Avoiding
5. Accommodating

Competing

This is when individuals pursue their own concerns at the other person's expense, using whatever it takes to win his or her position.

Collaborating

This is when individuals attempt to work with the other person to find a solution that fully satisfies the concerns of both.

Compromising

This is when the individuals' objective is to find a practical, mutually acceptable solution.

Avoiding

This is when the individual does not directly pursue his or her own concern or those of the other person; they do not address the conflict.

Accommodating

This is when the individual neglects his or her own concerns to satisfy the concerns of the other person; there is an element of self-sacrifice or "go along to get along."

Thomas-Kilmann describe that all types can be used depending on the circumstances:

- Competing—when there is an emergency and quick, decisive action is crucial.
- Collaborating—when you need to find an integrative solution and the concerns of both people are too important to be compromised.
- Compromising—when goals are moderately important but not worth the effort of the potential disruption involved in using more assertive modes.
- Avoiding—when an issue is unimportant or when other, more critical issues are pressing.
- Accommodating—when you realize that you are wrong, or to allow a better position to be considered, or to learn from others, and to show that you are reasonable.

The following diagram demonstrates this:

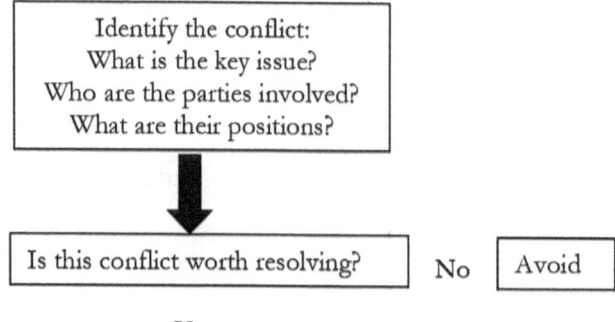

THE TOP FIVE THINGS TO CONSIDER BEFORE FILING AN EMPLOYEE RELATIONS COMPLAINT

Is it a policy or law that you must enforce?	Yes → Compete

No ↓

Is either outcome acceptable and the ongoing relationship of significant importance?	Yes → Accommodate

No ↓

Is this a major issue with enough time to reach a truly optimum solution?	Yes → Collaborate

If you are interested in more information and in taking the assessment, visit the following website: http://www.kilmanndiagnostics.com/.

Additionally, according to Scott (2009), the following are some things you may want to avoid:

- Turning this into a battle or war where you are going to win on this issue no matter what, where you are right and they are wrong.
- Looking for allies or people to agree and team up with you basically for a fight to win instead of a win-win.
- Creating and/or making assumptions.

The steps in the following diagram will also help keep you focused on your issue:

Author Unknown

Another great tool one may also want to consider is Stephen Covey's famous *7 Habits of Highly Effective People*:

Be Proactive

Address early on; don't wait until you start having pent-up anger and/or resentment.

Begin with the End in Mind

Again, what is your desired outcome? Best to think of how this can be a win-win for all.

Put First Things First

Make yourself aware of what is important and urgent and what is not important and not urgent.

THE TOP FIVE THINGS TO CONSIDER BEFORE FILING AN EMPLOYEE RELATIONS COMPLAINT

Think Win-Win

Value and respect people by understanding that a win for all is ultimately a better long-term resolution than if only one person in the situation had gotten his/her way.

Seek First to Understand Then to be Understood

Use good listening skills to genuinely understand a person, which compels them to reciprocate the listening and have an open mind to being influenced by you. This creates an atmosphere of caring and positive problem-solving.

Synergize

Try to find the common strengths you and the person bring to the team to make it successful. Remember, you were hired to utilize your skills, abilities, and knowledge to help the company be successful. Dragging the team down because things aren't going the way you think they should is a drain on the team and unproductive for the company.

Sharpen the Saw

Continue to do self-care in balancing and renewing your energy by continual exercise of your mind, body, and spirit. When any one of these areas is out of whack, it does not promote positive thinking.

*****

Finally, Scott (2009, p. 18) sums it up nicely: "Dealing with direct conflict isn't fun, even if you enjoyed plotting the next move to crush your opponent." It is an energy drainer, and coworkers, whether they are involved or not, start directing attention toward the person and their problems, and the work around is typically affected. It is good to work things out.

Additionally, it is good for you to keep in mind that you never know whom you'll be reporting to or who is weighing in on your next promotion.

One solution that doesn't work is being sneaky to get your way and beat the other person around the conflict. This doesn't really resolve the conflict; it may hold it off for a while, but it's likely that the person seen as the opponent will ultimately find a way to fight back. Perhaps it will be wise to figure out what you value or respect that is most important to you and practice ways to positively communicate that to your coworker.

Summary

WHEN IT COMES to potential company policy violations and/or illegal activity, we have a duty to act and they need to be reported. On the other hand, when it comes to employee conflicts, there are a lot of things to consider before filing a complaint. Notwithstanding, while it is important to raise your concerns in the workplace in either case, it is equally important to raise it in an effective manner that includes specific issues, clear outcomes, and respect for all parties involved. I cannot emphasize enough how critical it is to address issues early on so they don't turn into a war zone with the parties involved, and the expectation becomes for HR to enter the war zone and take sides and perhaps declare who won or is going to win the battle.

While HR strives to help resolve these conflicts, parties that have dug their heels in and are not satisfied until they win this war will spend a lot of time in their war zones, planning strategies for their next move, distracted from giving their maximum attention to their jobs and showcasing their work-related skills and abilities for which they were hired to do.

Typically, no one wins those battles; they usually end when one of the parties have moved on to something else, or worse circumstances, (e.g., stress, depression, disciplinary action, in some cases, termination for either party).

Referencing the top five things to consider before filing a complaint and how to file an effective complaint discussed in this book will help increase the chances of successfully resolving employee issues and concerns.

APPENDIX A

Answers to Scenario Questions in Chapter 4

Scenario 1

B. Employee conflict, not a policy violation leader should address

Scenario 2

B. No
Remember, while in the purest form of retaliation, it may meet retaliation; however, it does not meet the litmus test of illegal or a company policy violation because the employee filing the complaint must have filed a complaint against the leader, and the leader, in turn, conducted an adverse action of the employee's terms and/or conditions of employment (e.g., demotion, disciplinary action, termination).

Scenario 3

A. Illegal activity and/or policy violation
While not yet substantiated, it will be investigated as potential illegal activity and/or company violation.

Scenario 4

A. Illegal activity and/or company policy violation
While not yet substantiated, it will be investigated as potential illegal activity and/or company violation.

Scenario 5

A. Illegal activity and/or company policy violation
While not yet substantiated, it will be investigated as potential illegal activity and/or company violation.

Scenario 6

A. Illegal activity and/or company policy violation
While not yet substantiated, it will be investigated as potential illegal activity and/or company violation.

Scenario 7

B. Employee conflict, not an illegal activity or a company policy violation leader should address

Scenario 8

A. Illegal activity and/or company policy violation
While not yet substantiated, it will be investigated as potential illegal activity and/or company violation.

Notes

Preface

2017 Ethics and Compliance Hotline and Incident Management Benchmark Report, Navex Global Compliance (The Ethics and Compliance Experts). https://documents.akerman.com/2017EthicsandComplianceHotlineandIncidentManagementReport.PDF.

Introduction

"What Are Employee Relations?" https://www.hrzone.com/hr-glossary/what-are-employee-relations.
Muller, Debbie. 2014. "18 Surprising Employee Relations Statistics."
Equal Employment Opportunity Commission US. https://www.eeoc.gov/laws/statutes/index.cfm.
Scott, Vivian. 2009. *Conflict Resolution at Work for Dummies*.

Chapter 1

Lucas, Suzanne. 2014. "Moneywatch."

Chapter 2

Juliano, Lisa. 2015. "The Contemporary Psychoanalysis Group Contemporary Psychoanalysis in Action." https://www.psy-

chologytoday.com/blog/contemporary-psychoanalysis-in-action/201508/no-one-likes-complainer-heres-why.
Peanuts cartoon image https://www.bing.com/images/search?q=peanuts+comic+strip+1960+depression+stance&qpvt=peanuts+comic+strip+1960+depression+stance.
Pictures of venting https://www.bing.com/images/search?q=pictures+of+people+venting&id=0ADB2A5E22F52A4532FED0347C7DA81C0BE6D5B0&FORM=IQFRBA.
The Free Dictionary by Farlex. http://www.thefreedictionary.com/venting.
DuBois, Shelley. 2011. "Why Venting at Work Doesn't Help." http://fortune.com/2011/11/11/why-venting-at-work-doesnt-help/.

Chapter 3

Parris, Tamara. 2014. "Costs of Bullying—The Business Cost of Bullying in the Workplace." http://www.overcomebullying.org/costs-of-bullying.html.
Holladay, Hilary. 2013. "Self-Reflection: Are You a Workplace Bully?" http://www.workplacebullying.org/the-hook/.
Wikipedia, The Free dictionary, https://en.wikipedia.org/wiki/Workplace_incivility.
Bibi, Zainab, Karim, Jahanvash, and Siraj ud Din. 2013. "Workplace Incivility and Counterproductive Work Behavior: Moderating Role of Emotional Intelligence." *Pakistan Journal of Psychological Research, Islamabad* 28.2 (Winter): 317–334.

Chapter 4

Equal Employment Opportunity Commission US. https://www.eeoc.gov/laws/statutes/index.cfm.
FindLaw.com. http://statelaws.findlaw.com/civil-rights-laws.html.
US Equal Employment Opportunity Commission. https://www.eeoc.gov/eeoc/.

THE TOP FIVE THINGS TO CONSIDER BEFORE FILING AN EMPLOYEE RELATIONS COMPLAINT

Chapter 5-7

Selig, Meg. 2012. "The 9 Habits of Highly Effective Complainers." https://www.psychologytoday.com/blog/change-power/201203/the-9-habits-highly-effective-complainers.

U.S. Equal Opportunity Commission. "Time Limits for Filing a Charge." https://www.eeoc.gov/employees/timeliness.cfm.

Seltzer, Leon F. "6 Virtues and 6 Vices of Venting." https://www.psychologytoday.com/blog/evolution-the-self/201404/6-virtues-and-6-vices-venting.

"Skills You Need—Helping You Develop Life Skills." https://www.skillsyouneed.com/ips/effective-complaints.html.

"The 7 Habits of Highly Effective People." Wikipedia.

Scott, Vivian. 2009. *Conflict Resolution at Work for Dummies.*

Kenneth W. Thomas and Ralph H. Kilmann. 2007. "Thomas-Kilmann Conflict Mode Instrument."

John C. Maxwell. *The Maxwell Leadership Bible*, Revised and Updated (Lessons in Leadership from the Word of God).

Pictures

https://www.google.com/search?q=pictures+of+conflict+resolution+in+the+workplace&tbm=isch&tbs=rimg:CQUwhyPe7TZaIjjIe-cg1sG8h4o_1ZMwXHkMt0HyrKHnjZKqOhEVf0c_1b5EqoHfP1wo8rOovSYVlOgEMwianRDgogvSoSCch75yDWwbyHESNlyGc1gcNTKhIJij9kzBceQy0Rc1RgAXR0hQ0qEgnQfKsoeeNkqhFxiuxsLeFoCyoSCY6ERV_1Rz9vkEasNG5uQ5wIMKhIJSqgd8_1XCjysRSRuEz-BaYxsqEgk6i9JhWU6AQxF5aLUEoCapfioSCTCJqdEOCiC9EabKGbDrQ5NB&tbo=u&sa=X&ved=0ahUKEwiprNvM8KjWAhUo-jVQKHRRTCAsQ9C8IHw&biw=1536&bih=759&dpr=1.25#imgrc=BTCHI97tNlprpM.

https://www.bing.com/search?q=image+of+two+women+by+w.e.+hill&form=EDGEAR&qs=PF&cvid=9e32b8ed48374bd288482b515b1ab161&cc=US&setlang=en-US.

About the Author

PATRICE MILLER HAS approximately twenty years of experience in human resources (HR), including equal employment opportunity (EEO) and employee relations (ER), HR business consulting, and talent management. She has coached and trained hundreds of employees at all levels on performance management, leadership development, EEO/ER, change management, and conflict resolution.

She holds a bachelor's degree in HR management and a master's degree in industrial and organizational psychology. Patrice is a certified professional coach (CPC) from the Institute of Professional Excellence in Coaching (IPEC) and a certified energy leadership index master practitioner (ELI-MP).

Patrice founded DreamGoals Coaching LLC in October 2011, which offers performance-management coaching, leadership-development coaching, energy-leadership workshops, EEO and ER training, and conflict resolution.

www.ingramcontent.com/pod-product-compliance
Lightning Source LLC
Chambersburg PA
CBHW021042180526
45163CB00005B/2250